HUNGER'S TABLE

HUNGER'S TABLE

women, food
& politics

Margaret Randall

Papier-Mache Press
Watsonville, CA

01 00 99 98 97   5 4 3 2 1

ISBN: 1-57601-000-7 Softcover

Cover art by Dianne Sacchetti
Cover and interior design by Leslie Austin
Author photo by Marvin Collins
Copyediting by Cathey S. Cordes
Text composition by Leslie Austin
Proofreading by Shirley Coe
Manufactured by Malloy Lithographing, Inc.

Grateful acknowledgment is made to the following publications which previously published some of the material in this book, sometimes in an earlier version: "Antonio's Rice" in *New Letters;* "Battered Woman Surprise" in *Caprice;* "Bouillabaisse" in *American Voice;* "Buttermilk Bread" in *Sin Fronteras Journal* and *The Lucid Stone;* "Canyon Food" in *Ashes/Valley Arts Review of Scottsdale, Arizona;* "Cold Ginger Chicken" in *Prairie Schooner;* "Exorcism" in *The Lucid Stone;* "Hunger's Table" in *Visions-International;* "Mother's Chicken Soup" in *Women's Review of Books;* "Onion Soup" in *Prairie Schooner;* "Potato Latkes" in *Negative Capability;* "Sandra's Poor People's Recipes" in *Women's Review of Books;* and "The Staff of Life," "Cold Ginger Chicken," and "Bouillabaisse" in *Through the Kitchen Window: Women Writers on Hidden Hungers and Edible Traditions,* edited by Arlene Avakian (forthcoming from Beacon Press).

Library of Congress Cataloging-in-Publication Data
Randall, Margaret, 1936–
        Hunger's table: women, food, & politics / Margaret
Randall.
            p. cm.
        ISBN 1-57601-000-7 (softcover: alk. paper)
        1. Recipes—Poetry. I. Title.
PS3535.A56277H8   1996
811'.54—dc20
                                                96-30599
                                                CIP

*This book is dedicated with love
to my daughter Ximena
who inherited my engagement with cooking
and with words*

Contents

HUNGER'S
TABLE

Words of Warning

Women's relationship to food and cooking is bountiful and severe. It is natural as hope, comfortable as a mother's breast, weighed and measured, grubby and grand, fraught with desperation and made dangerous by desire. It is ritualized beyond the moon's lost light, yet remains an herb garden of possibility.

In Laura Esquivel's recent foreword to John Willoughby's cookbook, *An Appetite for Passion* (New York: Miramax Books, 1995), she generously applauds what she perceives as a new era in the cross-border empathy which the sharing of food cultures brings. "If we return to the cosmic," she writes, "we Mexicans are children of the maize, and people in the United States have eaten enough popcorn by now to be counted as kin." The coming together of peoples through the foods we eat is more and more a sign of our times. Globalization brings images of rampant starvation, increasing numbers of homeless people—even in countries like the United States—and the obscenely pampered tables of the super rich. But I am interested, as well, in the ways in which natural acts of eating are being challenged, distorted, camouflaged, or undermined by so many of society's wrong turns.

Our literature is beginning to reflect the deep contradictions. Peter Hoeg's new novel, *Smilla's Sense of Snow* (New York: Farrar, Straus & Giroux, 1993), contains several passages indicative of these incongruities. For example: "There are some women who can make soufflés. Who just happen to have a recipe for mocha parfait stuffed into their sports bra. Who can stack up their own wedding cakes with one hand and produce pepper steak Nossi Bé with the other. That ought to make all of us happy. As long as it doesn't mean that the rest of us have to have a guilty conscience because we're still not on a first-name basis with our toasters."

In this book, many of the poems are recipes, and the recipes poems. Each can be read for its experience and literary content, then, too, as one follows a page in a cookbook—with attention to all the details necessary for the confection of a thoroughly tested dish of food, salad, loaf of bread, dessert. Earlier in their birthings most contained full measure of their ingredients. When in public readings it became clear that this occasionally threatened the impact sought, I decided to provide such detailed instruction in separate notes.

Some poems address the preparation of food in unusual or unique circumstances. Others tell of dishes cooked by the women who precede us, those alter egos we continue to retrieve as we learn fully who we are. Some explore the relationship between eating and other of our daily tensions: hunger, racism, sexuality, body image, violence, the rampant abuse of women and children, breast cancer, AIDS, the blatant rise of fascism. Ours is a battered but resilient hope.

Gender defines our relationships to all these scenarios. Food and women, women and food. The sometimes nurturing sometimes uneasy place we make for food in our lives. And the prohibitions and demands that enter us like poison-tipped arrows, shot from the patriarchal bowstring. Often our private history remains a mass of unresolved conflict, more painful or contradiction filled than we are able to articulate. These poems are one woman's attempt to read between the menu's lines and to create a receptive language, free of coercion and danger.

How do we assimilate the bombardment of images: a skeletal child whose deadened eyes and pleading hands reach toward us from a country so distant to our experience…the Weight Watchers' silhouette, repeatedly straining against desire or even need…a commercial for stuffed-crust pizza followed by one for an exercise machine guaranteed to flatten that tummy or slim those thighs?

Looking back to a time before written history, men are referred to as the hunters, women as gatherers. The implication of such separateness continues to define who each of us learns to be. Yet there is something wrong with the succession of assumptions. Food gathering in preagricultural times *was* hunting. Women's relationship to what nurtures successive generations remains misunderstood, off balance.

In the United States as recently as the turn of this century, food was synonymous with home for the vast majority of women. For black women, that home frequently belonged to someone else—someone to whom they were linked by the most complex of exploitive relationships. Working- as well as middle-class men might order a drink or two at their local saloon and partake of its free buffet. Working women—many of them prostitutes—were also going to bars on both sides of the Atlantic. Soon their more aristocratic sisters began to have tearooms and a few restaurants, where they could eat in the company of men, but none where they were welcomed with other women, or alone.

So our foremothers shared their recipes with one another. Often written in a careful hand and passed from generation to generation, these histories are yet to be valued or even fully explored. Cooking and feeding are what we have always done. Poor women cooked for others. The wealthy hired cooks. In most places today, men remain the highly respected and well-paid chefs at expensive restaurants, while we women cook for our families and for others—although what, how, and under what circumstances varies greatly from culture to culture.

The images say a lot. A male restaurant chef appears immaculate in white, a traditional chef's hat increasing his height, his sensational irritability almost a requisite for fame. A woman is most often portrayed wiping her hands on a soiled apron as numerous small children pull at its hem. Yet she must struggle to be "perfectly groomed" and with dinner waiting when her husband returns from the world out there. In almost every language, the titles themselves describe dramatic difference: chef versus cook. Temperament versus drudgery. Thus gender intersects with class, race, and geographical location, further complicating a woman's relationship to food.

And it is not only the growing, gathering, preparation, and serving of food that is experienced by women in such different ways; what food does to us and what it means in our lives is an important part of the contemporary picture. Full-figured may still be a compliment in some cultures, where hunger is the human condition and fat is taken as a sign of prosperity. But increasingly, in middle- and upper-class America, the socially constructed emphasis on extreme thinness has provoked its own range of misery—and eating disorders.

At the broad base of the social pyramid, more and more women today live on welfare and support their children on its dwindling stipend. The assigning of food stamps includes a very particular language of abuse, which intimidates, denigrates, and controls even as it pretends to feed. Whatever her economic or social condition, an ordinary woman's real interaction with food is likely to stand in stark contrast to what she has been taught to expect—or the face she has been conditioned to put on it.

In this collection I bring together my own woman's voice and my love of cooking—mirrored halves of a powerfully female way of knowing. But I also bring issues about which it is more difficult to speak.

The first of these poems emerged explosively, almost no measurable distance from body cells to expressive lexicon. Then I began to urge them forth, drawing upon memory and myth; my complicated history with preparing, eating, and anguishing over food; dieting; and finally with the idea of just letting my body assume its natural size and shape. And all but a few of the poems have been created through laborious process—parallel to my ongoing struggle to occupy the physical territory of my life.

Like many women of my time and culture (born in 1936 in New York City, middle class, a shamefully assimilated Jew), I was an awkward child, then a self-consciously structured teenager. I hated physical education because it became a series of humiliations: finding myself alone on the playground when "chosen" last for the gym class team, suffering the jibes and laughter of my classmates when I missed a ball or stumbled as I tried to run. No one helped me find a sport I could like or do well, perhaps because no one believed it important. I was the girl who brought a doctor's note almost weekly, any excuse that would allow me to evade embarrassment.

Years passed in which I learned to choose the sedentary and the safe. I swam, then embraced the desert. Rode horses until I graduated to the understanding that this was a sport for the wealthy or a cowgirl's work. Developed an expert shot until the culture of violence became abhorrent to me. Team sports held too deep a memory of shame. I blamed my broadening hips on the writer's perennially seated position, grew heavier after the birth of my children, then imperceptibly—and eventually quite perceptibly—heavier as I aged. The physically inactive nature of my days and years left me with lax muscles and a thickening frame.

Oh, but I was adamant in defense of my body. Large—even fat—could indeed be beautiful. Why should I accept or internalize those messages issuing from a system I knew was profiting at my expense? But if I rejected conventional standards of appearance, I could not ignore the fact that I felt less and less in touch with my body and less able to move the way I wished. The evidence was closing in from without, as well as from an internal history now opening like a flower.

In midlife, I entered a relationship with a woman who biked, who had climbed mountains, and who loved white-water canoeing or just floating down a river. She adored my ample body. The first time we rode bikes together, I managed two city blocks. Instead of the scorn I'd been conditioned to expect, she said: "Well, that was terrific. You did *great!*" I *wanted* to try again. Our biking soon ran to ten- or twenty-mile mornings. I'd discovered the first of several sports that now give me pleasure.

One day at age fifty-five while Barbara and I were riding along an Albuquerque bike trail, I turned to her and said, "I can't stand this anymore. I can't do the diets. I can't keep the promises. I want to start going to a gym." Typical of our life together, she immediately took on the challenge as her own. A rigorous exercise program, which has now become a welcome and integral part of our living, along with a modest reduction of excess fat in our diet, moved me five sizes down the clothing scale more quickly than I'd imagined possible.

Clearly, other issues had also come into focus at that point, and these too had begun to change me at the cellular level. My children had grown and my nurturing of them had become more spiritual, less immediate. I discovered the history of incest perpetrated by my maternal grandfather and worked to come to terms with its memory. Menopause brought me to a new and powerful place. I struggled with the decision to leave the extraordinary countries where I'd lived for a quarter century and return to my roots in the southwestern United States. A deportation order pushed me to reaffirm my deepest belief in justice, and the resultant political battle gave generously of its solidarity even as it depleted me emotionally. I also embraced my lesbian identity.

In these disparate but deeply connected travels, I retrieved enough of myself to be able to break with a few destructive patterns. The time was right for change. Now I can nod my head without fighting folds of flesh beneath my chin. I stretch and hike and enjoy other activities that once seemed too difficult—or beyond my reach. But the struggle is never ending. I do not believe it is accidental that these poems emerged after several years of having been able to alter my diet and stick to a daily workout, after I'd become more comfortable with the intake and meaning of food in my life. And in a time in which food has become a marker—whole nations of peoples starving, unimaginable opulence on the tables of the rich, a slender silhouette crowding the dominant culture's message for success (especially in this country and especially for women)—the work is unlike anything I have seen. Or anything I have done before.

Today I would still describe myself as a large woman forever on the edge of neurotic eating—but one who is healthier, happier with her body image, and who writes passionate poems about food. "The Climb" offers a very explicit view of the relationship between my mastery of new physical activities and my changing approach to eating. Although less marked, this process can be felt in many of the other poems as well. Reading and thinking about food, preparing it for myself and others, working out or hiking the foothills where I live, and producing this collection are all lines that collide and pull apart, parallel one another, and then merge again.

I am a nonreligious (but deeply spiritual) socialist, a Jewish lesbian in my late fifties, a writer, a photographer, and a political activist. Mother of four, grandmother of six. I was born in New York City and lived almost half my adult life in Latin America, in Mexico, Cuba, and Nicaragua. And so my culinary culture is varied. It surfaces through memories of childhood family favorites. It can be found in the dishes I learned to prepare in my artist's poverty of the late fifties or during several marriages throughout the sixties and seventies; while living under severe rationing in Cuba (1969–80); and while engaged in revolutionary struggle in Nicaragua (1980–84). And it reappears, embellished, in response to my own children's and grandchildren's pleas.

The poems combine a generosity of taste, scent, and color with imagery and craft. Through their fabric are woven the obstinate threads of a lifelong quest for social justice, the New Mexican desert which nurtures my heart, midlife humor, and the love of one woman for another. Most of the recipes are originals; where this is not the case, or where other references must be made to explain a person, dish, or situation, credit is given in the notes. They have been tested and retested. I vouch for them, and so do my family and friends.

Cookbooks? I am crazy about them. Everywhere I go I find myself looking for old or unusual ones, and I read them like the diaries and histories they are. They not only occupy a shelf in my kitchen, but also sit on my night table and are taken with me when I travel. Others may curl up with a good novel; these days I find secrets and energy in both exotic and mundane recipes.

A list of such collections would be much too long to enumerate here. Besides, I am always finding new ones. But I will mention two books about food and the politics of recipe collecting: *Food in History* by Reay Tannahill (New York: Crown Publishers, 1988) and *America's Collectible Cookbooks* by Mary Anna DuSablon (Athens: Ohio University Press, 1994). During the writing of these poems, both books provided points of departure, or filled in gaps in my knowledge of how food cultures have developed.

In Albuquerque, I am part of a group of women writers who have been meeting for almost five years to share and critique one another's work. Monthly gatherings are also potlucks, for which the woman who hosts the gathering prepares a main dish and the others bring bread, wine, salad, dessert, or some additional delicacy. We rarely check in with one another beforehand, yet these dinners are always delightfully balanced. We've often said that we'll have to put together a cookbook of our own one day!

And so I owe a great deal to Paula Gunn Allen, Nancy Gage, Janice Gould, Minrose Gwin, Ruth Salvaggio, Patricia Clark Smith, Sharon Warner, and Mimi Wheatwind, whose discerning sensibilities about food and the written word helped birth many of these poems. My partner, Barbara Byers, read and commented on all of them, often through interminable drafts. She has long been my most severe and loving critic.

My brother John Randall deals in old and rare books; I'm grateful for his generosity. He has unearthed and offered up several fascinating texts. My dear friend and immigration lawyer, Michael Maggio, himself a splendid cook, was ready with helpful suggestions. Thanks, also, to those friends who have eaten at our table and have been brave enough to critique the dishes themselves; as well as to the many who have shared their own recipes, notations, ideas, and references to lost or out-of-print resources.

I hope this book will speak to several audiences: to poetry lovers, cookbook devotees, and men as well as women who appreciate the intersections of these forces in our lives. This is a collection that defies boundaries, inviting the reader to a place just beginning to be mapped by those of us who suffer as we taste, grow as we devour our way through the body's knowledge.

—Albuquerque, Summer–Winter 1995

Cold Ginger Chicken

Round tables gather a family in, reject
a father who commands the head, a mother
running to and from the kitchen
as courses replace one another
and conversations wane.

Mix fresh grated ginger, 4 cloves
grated garlic, rock salt
and olive oil. When sauce has blended,
cover and refrigerate at least 2 hours.
Square or rectangular tables

arrange and order a family, there is always
one who must keep her back to the wall,
another who cannot take direct sunlight
or naturally occupies the end
from which directives flow.

Boil chicken breasts about 10 minutes or
until just barely cooked. Remove from heat
and plunge into ice water. Skin. Cover
with plastic wrap and chill. When cold,
cut into 2-inch pieces. Arrange on a bed

of watercress, leaving a space in the center
for your bowl of sauce. One side, each end,
center or gentle diameter. Position
is everything when winter comes
and snow begins to fall.

Ingredients
1/2 cup fresh grated ginger
4 cloves grated garlic
1 teaspoon rock salt
1 cup olive oil

Grape Pie

1

This pie calls for 4 cups blue grapes
and asks that skillful fingers
slip the pulp from their skins.
It requires you cook the lush mass
until its seeds loosen,
and begs you keep your fantasies in check.

Press cooked pulp through a colander
to remove but save the seeds. Your
breathing stumbles now, mouth dries,
thighs tingle and body moves
gently back and forth.

Now combine the pulp, seeds,
sugar, lemon juice,
grated orange rind,
and quick-cooking tapioca.
These ingredients must stand 15 minutes
while you line a pie plate with dough
and preheat your oven to 450 degrees.

Fill the shell with the deep blue mixture
and form a lattice across the top.
Bake 10 minutes hot
and 20 more at medium heat.

2
But wait.

Listen for the voices of César's people
in the grape fields of California.
If you hear them striking
you must refuse to serve or eat this pie.

Ingredients
4 cups blue grapes
3/4 cup sugar
1 1/2 tablespoons lemon juice
1 tablespoon grated orange rind
1 tablespoon quick-cooking tapioca

Bouillabaisse

You may use roughy or filet of sole,
delicate white fish flaking tender
to the nudge of fork
or old hunger.
Set aside the loaves and fishes
of our several memories.
Open your mouth. Wide. The world
crawls beneath your tongue.
Speak of famine and human need.
Nothing will disappear
before your breath quickens
and wise women sit at your table.

Cut the raw filets into bite-size pieces
and place them in a dish
already graced with large bay scallops.
Close your eyes. Remember your childhood dreams
of justice and deserved reward.
A steady stream of cool water
soothes your fingers
as they rinse and peel the shells
from large green shrimp. Twenty or 30.
They too go into the dish,
a mound of clean cold products of the sea.

Stop everything. Stand very still.
Think of the perfect dinner guest.
Her clear eyes look back at yours,
acknowledging the feast to come.
You might want snapper or salmon
though the latter will make a heavier soup.
Add mussels in their obsidian shells.
Bits of crab are delicacies.
Rings of cleaned squid
unusual and satisfying.

The dish of fresh seafood and fish
goes into the white refrigerator,
waits while we keep looking away
from those pictures of the world's starving,
deadened limbs reaching out,
eyes larger than the faces in which they shine.
Refuse to hold the images
without their counterpart of culture—
people making and doing.
Who are they?

And still they starve. And still,
this is how we prepare to eat—
accepting them clean of their history,
their halved voice.
In a deep soup pot heat 1/4 cup olive oil.
Add 1/2 cup finely chopped onion,
stirring until translucent but not browned.
Throw in 8 or 10 plump garlic cloves,
peeled and minced.

A teaspoon dark red saffron strands,
a teaspoon grated orange rind,
another of freshly ground white pepper,
and a tablespoon finely chopped fresh fennel.
A pinch of celery or fennel seed,
a bit of basil.
Stir in 4 to 5 peeled tomatoes
and 2 or 3 tablespoons tomato paste.
A cup chopped fresh parsley is optional,
your garden earth.

And finally salt, that lively grain of the sea—
a couple of teaspoons, or to taste.
Stir often.
We are almost ready now.
Our hands almost touch,
reaching across an ocean of greed and ache,
claiming the images in these eyes,
ours and theirs. We are almost finished
pretending they are not part of us,
or we of them.

To the vegetables add 6 cups fish stock
or water, and allow to simmer an hour or so
until the soup is eaten.
Five minutes before you bring it to table
add the fish and seafood,
stirring over a raised flame
until they are just done.
Pink shrimp, scallops an opaque white
—tender but never overcooked.

Ladle the bouillabaisse over thin slices
of toasted garlic bread, one to a bowl,
or accompany with steamed white rice.
The bowls may be cobalt blue
or cadmium red.
Green salad or creamed spinach,
white wine, fresh pears with hot brie
make a good dessert.
Nothing will chide us
but those great eyes staring
from the bottom of pot or plate,
a numbed request where nothing but silence
stood.

Play discreet music now,
or garnish with lively conversation,
unrehearsed.

Potato Latkes

There is nothing quite like this taste,
my hand and mouth,
a winter evening in Manhattan.
You have given yourself a treat
because the uptown editor said no

to your first shy novel, because
he looked you over
benevolent behind his drink
and said go back to Albuquerque
get married and oh yes

have some kids. No one lives
where he wants you to go.
Steam rises from subway grates
and frost splits the atom
of this hunger strafed by memory.

Only a square of waxed paper
separates your fingers
from the sizzling batter,
just short of crisp but never soggy—
grated potatoes wrung dry
inside the clean white cloth,
three of them tossed with
flour, cream, some
grated onion, a beaten egg
and salt to taste.

Today I coat the skillet with
butter or bacon grease,
spoon the mixture to pancake size
and turn until golden
on each side.

Now I serve them with homemade
applesauce or sour cream.
Back then I paid for food
on the run, walked fast, dreamed
of ancestors who never used

the fat of swine. Those years
I devoured calendar and sustenance,
acknowledged a link
between the woman I imagined myself to be
and 14th Street's neon rush,

voices that begged: Sit down,
take a load off, stay a while.
I couldn't hear the meaning
of those words, didn't know
about Hannah, sister of Aaron

whose eyes took the camera defiant
and looked so much like mine.
Now I sit and eat, ponder
the apple-green sauce
or glistening sour of thick cream

against the crisscross gold.
I understand the words
and how they made me who I am.
We eat together slowly now.
Together and slowly.

Ingredients
3 peeled and grated potatoes wrung dry in a clean cloth
1 tablespoon flour
1 tablespoon cream
1/2 grated onion
1 beaten egg
salt to taste

Shirley's Kugel

Shirley's kugel takes 2 tablespoons butter,
1/2 pound creamed cottage, and 1/2 pound
cream cheese. I know, already there's
nowhere you can hide

doing battle with such fare,
cholesterol booster for the ages.
But wait, there's more: 5 eggs,
1 1/4 cups sugar, 1 pint milk,

and another of sour cream. A deep sigh
rises from your throat, resignation
grabs your fallen shoulders
and still this is not the end:

a teaspoonful of vanilla, a sprinkle
of cinnamon, and handful of raisins,
all of it generous as the breast
you wished your mother had gathered you to,

the dreams that fold themselves around
a fear so small it's musical score
is a single Andean pipe. Klezmer,
you chide, believing I confuse

the sound this chorus brings.
But I tell you
our dance follows no geographical line
and urge you continue with 2 tablespoons

melted butter and half a pound thin noodles
cooked and reserved for last. After
preheating your oven to 350 degrees
and greasing a large flat pan

with half the melted butter, mix
all ingredients but the noodles.
Blend until fairly smooth. Then add
the noodles and raisins, stirring gently

until the mixture sings your name.
Pour into pan. Then top with remaining
butter and sprinkle with cinnamon.
Bake one hour or until the kugel is firm.

Finally take from the oven and cut
in little squares. Offer with eager hands,
leaning slightly into the serve,
an expression of bewilderment

upon your eyes. Your guests will come back
for more. No one will gain an ounce,
and all their dreams
will be forgotten when they wake.

Battered Woman Surprise

A recipe for baba ghannouj, a Near Eastern blend of baked eggplant, tahini, parsley, garlic, and lemon, often served with wedges of pita bread.

The great round purplish black eggplant
is quietly crazed in loneliness.
Not merely alone or needing space
but lonely in its full circumference.
Floating, burgundy, swollen in fear.

Prick her all over with the tines of a fork
then lay her directly on the rack
of an oven set to 400. In 45 minutes
she will shrink into herself, her polished skin
a defeated mass of wrinkles.

When cool enough to handle, scrape her flesh
to a bowl with 1/4 cup sesame tahini,
lots of pressed garlic, finely chopped
parsley, salt, pepper, and the juice
from at least two lemons.

Now her blue-black sheen is gone, her fullness
barely remembered. But this delicacy
—chilled aphrodisiac—
may be scooped into a little center bowl
surrounded by Wheat Thins or melba toast.

Before serving, drizzle a bit of olive oil
across the top. Guests will enjoy
the exotic taste you share with them.
And the appetizer—improved for its own good—
will not complain.

Mother's Chicken Soup

We weren't even nominal Jews, I mean
we were Jews who had excised
the nominal, routed in generations
before and beyond my birth.
Uprooted. Name changed. Cut from the vine.

Still, today I wheeze my way
through dreams of chicken soup,
the healing steam of its aroma
nudging the soreness of my nostrils,
balls of matzo bobbing in each bowl.

At fifty I ask for broth when I am sick,
wait for patient hands
to bring it on a tray
where I'm down in fever or in pain.

I'll even settle for Jell-O now.
Risk the phone. Plead with Mother
to bring some over.
Anything to soothe this raging throat.

Her recipe is hit and flee the scene.
She rings the bell, then leaves
an unopened Jell-O box upon my stoop.
Her precaution against the germs.

Run, Mother, run.

The Great American Cafeteria Line

Gripping your tray you notice
evidence of sterile wash,
and lighter images come to mind.

Ahead, the after-churchers,
father's paunch,
a sculptured slab
of chicken-fried steak
and mound of mashed potatoes
so white the gravy pools
are two-toned on its pasty mass.
Aluminum taste of waxed green beans,
or ketchup as that extra vegetable.

Any of this fresh?
The silly question floats.
A tiny dish of brussels sprouts
leans forward to respond,
then dies on overcook.

This sends you back to safer options—
salads—and you choose
the orange of shredded carrot,
glistening pineapple, plastic tufts
of baby marshmallow

until—a human conveyor now—
you're pulled along once more,
wondering which and if and how
these picture-perfects taste.

All you can eat?
A cashier whose mask belies
her less than minimum wage,
two babies at home, and a man
who expects his on the table,

chats your items,
guesses you'll pay less
for one-on-one,
then calls the dollars in and turns
to the family of six
appearing 'round the bend.

They've taken full advantage
of America's best.
What you see is what you get.

Key lime pie.
Brush back the perky smile.
Devour,
and be done.

Canyon Food

for Dennise Gackstetter

"The first day I make too much food,"
you tell me.
"That lets people know they can come back for more.
Then they eat what they want, aren't anxious
about getting enough.
I have less waste and a measure of appetites."

Dennise, I have asked for your secrets,
how you learned to cook for twenty-four campers
forging 286 miles of furious river
through 1.7 billion years of wind and rock,
three thousand of human culture
and our own sixteen days.

You explain how everything has to be packed in,
all waste taken out.
I have seen each pristine campground welcome us,
done my part to leave them unspoiled
for travelers to come.

River water filtered through porcelain
when we drink,
pumped into pans or shot through with Clorox
when used to clean the dishes and mugs.
Long metal tables
that circumscribe your kitchen,
doubling as hatch covers,
waiting as backboards in case of emergency.

I have noticed your daily squares of paper,
lists for each boatman
to forage for boxes of lettuce,
bags of chicken breasts, apples in buckets,
Oreo cookies and cheese,
coffee, vegetables, chocolate, clams.

Mike growing sprouts in the bottom of his dory.
Mary hauling silver tanks of butane.
The exuberance
of Shawn's fried fish tacos.
Jano putting her lips to a blue plastic toy,
sacred "trombat" calling us to dinner.

"It's all in the timing," you say,
"all about knowing how long
to simmer the rice,
when to light a fire beneath the vegetables
or set the salmon steaks to broil."
Hot coals cover your Dutch oven
raised on flattened beer cans, promise
of dessert again tonight.

"It's all in the timing."
You grin.
And I know you mean
this mammoth scale
slowing us down
allowing us to drift
from that constraint we call civilization,

trusting ourselves to fall backward
into our deepest appetites.

The Climb

Small steps now. One foot before
the other, and don't forget
to breathe. But slowly.
Arizona sun
polishes the old ribs of
tough-skinned saguaros.
November's new leaves flicker
along the ocotillo's slender arms.
We wonder what moisture
brings them out,
so long past the monsoons of August.

I have not thought
of the carrot and a half
we scraped and cut to
do for three,
the homemade hummus and
black bread, an apple each.
Not once have images of food
beckoned between the dust
that rises off this rocky trail
and my determined tread.

Wasson hides somewhere beyond
the next switchback
or the one after that.
I suck a gurgle of dry air
from my Camelback
and refuse to dwell
on the long descent.
Then the visitor's book
stares up at me.
I've "bagged my first peak"
as the competitors say.

The rock is sweet against
my thighs.
Hummus on black bread, faint
savor of garlic on my tongue.
A bite of carrot,
apple down to the core.
It is not hunger that pulls
these edibles to my lips,
replaces craving with enough.
For me it's never been
only hunger, fullness of enough.

Climbing has taken my vertigo and
placed it on some other canyon rim,
taken gluttony and pushed it
from the trail.
Climbing has given me food
as nourishment, not safety or reward.
Bolting down this mountain
as I labored up,
I run my laughing tongue
over the stubborn salt of fear.

Rhetorical Rhubarb

for Barbara

One day your inch-thick life moves placidly
beside you. Then the word
malignant
drops in your hands
and your living is ten feet down,
so dark in the depths
you cannot see or even feel your toes.

One day you wonder at your joy,
the world devours itself
and you believe you must savor its pain
in steady mouthfuls.
How can I escape the war around me,
you ask, how do I grow?

Then you taste the bitter
in long chewy strands,
pepper stings your eyes,
nothing will be the same.
Can there be time
to wash the pink stems,
a color for which there are no words?

Will there be space to speak
what you might have said
with all the time
to gaze upon your lover's naked shoulders
of an autumn afternoon?
Start now.
Clean the long stalks
of their earthy grit.

If they are old, peel back
the toughest strings.
Never use the leaves
as they are heavy in oxalic acid.
Four cups unpeeled young rhubarb stalks
diced, then flour, sugar, butter,
and a whiff of powdered orange rind.

Add fresh strawberries
cut so their juices flow.
This mixture is placed in a pie shell
with latticed top or crust.
You may brush it with egg and a bit of milk
before baking 20 minutes at 350 degrees
and another 20 at 400.

Now they have cut the malignancy away.
Only our years will tell
if you've used
what you earned.

Ingredients
4 cups unpeeled diced young rhubarb stalks
1/4 cup all-purpose flour
1 1/2 cups sugar
1 tablespoon butter
dash of powdered orange rind
4 cups fresh strawberries
enough pie dough for a 2-crust pie

Squash Blossom Budín

This is a recipe from The Blue House, though filtered
through another woman's hands.
There were women all over Frida's kitchen,
in her bedroom too
though she remained the centerpiece—
a raging fire.

Squash Blossom Budín serves twelve who come to dance
at the alter of her spirit.
Coatlicue—necklace of skulls,
mother who ate her children
before she would see them slaves.

No children from Frida's life, but we
who are threatened or challenged
take refuge in this history of dangerous foods.
Come. The table
is set, the cast iron stove
awaits our braided hands.

Prepare the crepes. These require
butter, eggs, flour, and milk.
Over your left shoulder, a toss of salt.
Additional butter coats the skillet
before you swirl a tablespoon of batter
into its yawning belly.

Mere seconds on either side. Remove the crepes,
placing a square of waxed paper between each
as it, impatient, waits.
Sauté a finely chopped onion
until a window opens upon Frida's time
and you follow your broken words
all over her kitchen walls.

Add the yellow blossoms whose stems and pistils
have been discarded.
Salt and pepper sing a high duet.
You must cook this 4 or 5 minutes
before adding pureed tomatoes,
and let it simmer until the mixture
is thick enough to fill the crepes.

By now you have lost whole bodies of words.
A silence fills your veins, your eyes
circle the images that drag their muted names
across this counter top.

Frida's words are locked in her painted journal,
low-pitched and fierce. Her colors
did not go until she abandoned them,
sidestepping what is not easy in life:
it will return.

Tired of obligation, you line a green and brown
baking dish with one layer of crepes,
another of filling, another
of grated Oaxaca or Muenster cheese.
Repeat.
Again, repeat.

Bake at 350 degrees until the crepes
are hot and the cheese is bubbly and smooth.
The words are all gone now.
Will no one know what you meant to say?

Still, a savor of squash blossom
holds healing court
at the fragile shoreline of your tongue.

Ingredients
Crepes
4 tablespoons melted butter
6 eggs
3/4 cup flour
3/4 cup milk
salt

Filling
1 finely chopped onion sautéed in 2 tablespoons butter
2 pounds squash blossoms
1 1/2 cups pureed tomatoes

Soft Pretzels

Sudden movement slams your heart,
ricochets off the inner walls
of a body you imagine wet
and dark, a cave where machinery
grinds to a halt, inevitably.

This is as simple as forty years ago
when a question wasn't itself
and you had yet to learn your name.
Soft pretzels are made
with a cup of warm water, 105

to 115 degrees, a package of yeast,
2 tablespoons sugar, 1 teaspoon salt,
1 tablespoon softened butter
and roughly 3 1/2 cups flour.
Mix all ingredients

to form a resilient dough, then set
to rise in a greased bowl.
After 40 minutes, roll out, modeling
your pretzels as you would little bows
of clay or Plasticine, then let these

rise again on a greased sheet.
Lastly brush each bow
with a mixture of egg yoke
beaten with water,
and sprinkle with coarse rock salt.

Bake for 15 minutes at 350 degrees.
Someone is watching your hands
as they work the dough,
she follows the movement of little bows
from counter top to metal sheet.

You brush a tumble of stuttering hair
from your damp face.
Someone will ask you
where these years have gone,
who you believed you would be

back then, where you were headed.
Someone else will laugh at the question,
knees gathered to chest
in a dusty corner on the floor
humming a melody you only remember

when you close your eyes. The scent
of warm dough stills your heart,
a sudden movement
turns your attention back in time,
revives a thunderous pulse.

Ode to Velveeta

Because I thought my mother the most
beautiful, perfect in every way,
I loved her spaghetti baked
with thick slabs of Velveeta,
a rubberized gel, chemical taste
and crusty overburn.

Because I believed her smart and that Dad
knew everything, the green plastic bowl
was mine at breakfast or for supper's stew.
Toastites pressed and molded
white bread with its mound of tuna fish,
Velveeta again through eager teeth.

My mother did not cultivate the kitchen,
women's enslavement to the family
in her sense of it.
She did not bake, never produced warm cookies
after school, offered her smattering of dishes,
their tastes gone now in more sophisticated fare.

Sale-priced drum of powdered milk, bloody eggs
and horse meat "cheaper than ground round"
were money savers
just as home-colored margarine was patriotic
in the war effort of my childhood,
sales coupons clipped from every daily paper.

Like the other girls of my time I was
designed for marriage
but nobody taught me how to cook.
All these years later,
past children and grandchildren of my own,
my kitchen is art studio and science lab.

Cooking does not enslave
but sets me free.

Macaroni Au Gratin

Aw *graa*tin or ow grat*een*, the great
American filler. Take
1 1/2 cups macaroni
break into 1-inch lengths (the modern
supermarket has these packaged to go).
But *The New Cookery* by Lenna Frances Cooper
director of the Battle Creek Michigan
Sanitarium School of Home Economics, 1929,
includes all the instructions
we will ever need.

"Cook macaroni in boiling salted water
until tender, then drain
and pour over it a dash of cold."
Jenny Craig squeals, embraces
the "after" woman whose "before" image
remains unwanted and sad
at the corner of our TV screen,
a constant reminder:
there but for the grace of fortitude
go you and you and I.

Do not turn away as you make a white sauce
of butter and flour, milk, and a touch of salt.
Mix with the cooked macaroni.
Turn the volume up, but not the heat.

Walk, do not run. Jog, do not walk
in your mix-matched halter and sweats.
Stir in a cup of yogurt
or grated Neufchâtel cheese.

Turn this mixture into a baking dish
and cover with bread crumbs.
Bake in a moderate oven until nicely browned.
Off a pound, on a pound, off a pound, ten.
Or seventy.

Cook and eat and watch and cook and eat.
Note:
if desired, buttered crumbs may be used.

Ingredients
1 1/2 cups macaroni
4 quarts boiling salted water
3 tablespoons butter
3 tablespoons flour
2 cups milk
1 teaspoon salt
1 cup yogurt or grated cheese
1 cup bread crumbs

Spaghetti Lure

Our first date I baked a delicate soufflé,
fresh salmon flaked and fluffed
in seasoned egg whites
beaten to just the right consistency
of casual desire.
New peas. Imported cheese.

A simple dish, advertising constancy
beyond the one-night stand.
You ate and smiled and later
asked if we might not be more comfortable
on the bed.

We'd been together several years
when you admitted
you hate soufflés of any kind.

I sautéed dainty chicken livers
simmered in red wine
with a savor of onion and garlic,
the heft of new potatoes
roasted golden in scant measure of oil.

But you say you hate liver,
filter of all
that is excess and waste.

I labored over crepes
thin as the strudel
made by a grandmother I never had,
filled them with exotic vegetables
and ordinary song.

But the sauce in those crepes
churns your stomach,
reminds you of places you cannot return
and do not want to be.

Spaghetti, you plead,
embarrassed
by such singular desire.

I part sun-dried tomatoes
with my kitchen shears,
add camouflaged eggplant
and bright red peppers
to penne regate, vary
with shells or bow tie or lasagna,
suggest pesto
fresh from a friend's garden,
invent an Alfredo sauce
that honors this new year
and all its possibilities.

But no. You want plain linguini
with only "red sauce."
Perhaps a dash of parmesan
if adventurous.

Spaghetti lure: you could eat it
and be happy every night.
Yet I continue to insist on difference,
experiment with diversity,
cleave you hard
to my culinary need.

Cleora's Dream

Cleora Butler grew up near Muskogee, Oklahoma,
daughter of a generous black family.
She wanted to be a cook.
Muskogee surrounds me
in dreams where my Creek poet friend

takes me by the hand.
We round a corner.
I never glimpse
what lies beyond that turn
but move with a flute of knowledge
on my skin.

Cleora did cook, for rich white folks
who loved and paid her well.
She learned to make hats
when forced to try one on
in the back room of a millinery shop
where white society did not have to watch.
Had her own bakery and catering business
in Tulsa "when the race began to thrive."

Her brother Walter played saxophone
with Cab Calloway's orchestra
of Cotton Club fame.
She nursed her father-in-law
and then her husband,
wrote her recipes down.

Cleora tells a story of pride
and banquet elegance,
of grit and narrow purpose.
Granddaughter of slaves,
on Indian land she teaches a culture
beyond her streets, those storefronts,
her patron's mansions
turned public gathering place.

Unfinished movement into time.
Of home-brewed vinegar,
she says from the 1870s on
women-shared "receipts"
such as this one
from *Woman's Favorite Cookbook*:

"Put in an open cask
four gallons of good cider
and one of molasses,
cover the top with thin muslin
and leave it in the sun,
bringing it in at night
and when it rains.

In four weeks you will have vinegar
sharp enough for any tongue."

Second Vinegar Poem

In the vinegar jar beneath
your grandmother's kitchen sink,
the floating mass of white
was called the "Mother."
Starter for amber gallons of liquid,
pungent yet clean. Mysterious ghost.

I remember the morning
we scattered Father's ashes
among the juniper and cholla.
On the photograph's surface
a small white cloud,
discernible image of the man.

Warning: against possible contamination,
scrub all utensils well.
Dry thoroughly.
Keep jars in a cool dark place.
Like some mysterious ghosts,
our births and deaths
refuse to be contained.

Over Easy

Imprisoned within the egg,
yoke and white
square off for spring.

What happens at earthquake zero?
First crack
initiates a landslide,

second brings images,
a story we believed
would never come to our house.

The perfect omelette,
or sunny-side up
with sausages and fries.

Pale scent of virgin oil
or stench
of a sour griddle.

Imprisoned inside the shell
yoke and white
compete.

When will we find a way
to truly know those different from ourselves?

Antonio's Rice

It was plain white rice, scant ration of salt
to move us on. Cuba, the revolution's glory years
and still we had five pounds a month, a lot
you'll say, but think of it there on the plate
with nothing adorning its size.

He served it up in little mounds, formed by
filling one light green plastic coffee cup
then inverting its equity before each patient fork.
An egg or some *butifarra* (hot dog-like sausage,
occasional treat) if things were good,

a ladle full of split pea soup if they were not.
How we joked about those split peas,
chícharos in every possible disguise.
Boil and throw the water out, boil again
and throw out the water, and again and again

until the punch line telling you to throw out
the peas. And also the pot.
Carmen whispered that version one early dawn
as we patrolled the block, arms swinging in unison,
collars raised against cold sea air.

Women keeping our neighborhood safe against crime,
invasion, or loneliness,
whatever threatened that nation
of spent cooks. Tomato sauce without tomatoes.
Marmalade made from boiling the mango skins.

Those hours the recipes came—an endless volley
against the dark sea wall, back and forth
between neighbors struggling to stay awake.
Antonio's rice was the stalwart,
the sure thing,

guaranteed to bring that beautiful fairness
into our home.

Migration of Seasons

The Torah calls it "causeless hatred"
—Malka Drucker

1
Raw beneath the terrible fangs of Master Race,
I wade a blueprint of astonishment:
the Nazis' protection of animals
webbed counterpoint to their murder
of Jews, Romas, Bolsheviks, queers.
Mysteries that erode our safety even now.

Recalling to mortal pain not only the Nazi
—festering, othered by what remains of history—
but all of us, poised upon our symmetry
of indignation.
Those who would save the seals and ignore humanity,
save the fetus and kill the woman—kidnapped, borrowed, bought.

The world must not forget, we said, when evidence
raised its gaunt hands in surrender.
Yet we did forget, or never knew Hitler and Goebbels,
Himmler and Hess sought the blond beast in man,
used women to revive those Nordic genes
as they named kosher butchers unspeakably cruel.

Exalt the stag, the elk and wild boar, cherish Blondi
the wolfhound, swift whippet or faithful German shepherd
bred until its hind legs tremble in obedience.
The hunt was never sport for the elite
who sent humanity to ovens, boxcars
still begging landscape in our eyes.

Abstinence from meat was membership in that club,
a migration of seasons returning to haunt us
as we sleep. Monuments rising today
on commemorative sites
deposit memory where it will not interfere
with the way we eat or dream or use our animals.

Now I speak to and of us all: we and the always-other
still dreaming of freedom from their choices,
still striving to suffer from themselves
as others have suffered from them.
March 22, 1938: Jews forbidden to grow vegetables.
May 15, 1942: Jews forbidden to own pets.

Entries on a calendar of inquisitional news,
each ban made easier by acceptance
of what came before. Scourge of the deliberate life.
How to keep faith as those who remember die,
when memory itself is judged
unlawful or untrue?

2
Across that South Valley yard
an almost human shriek
pierced juniper air,
a sound as new as this place
we'd come to—Albuquerque 1947.

I shrank and looked to my father
who looked at his own blunt hands
aged on the cello's neck and bow.
They would fold and fall
before they harmed the life of any species.

Our family traveled west, its Jewishness denied
and rattling from jaw to jaw. Brought only
our own long line of gentle German shepherds.
Desire for a different life.
Fear of authority. Dis-ease with truth.

Then suddenly it was Dad and me in the farmyard
choosing our turkey live.
I demanded answers and he had none
though surely he would have given
me the world, his gentle heart.

I won't eat it, I told him then, too pierced
by the sound, too hurt, and don't remember
what I feasted, on Thanksgiving of my eleventh year,
how long my protest burned,
or how accommodation coaxed me home.

Now I repeat my litany of Thanksgivings—fetish
or murder in a life that calls them back,
away from the knife
thrust down that garbled throat,
cleansed of the holiday smile,

names dropped in the gravy boat,
a family that comes together once a year,
seeking the full embrace
where bodies rest
and animal-to-human is continuum.

3
A lion's print upon wet sand, bear scat
profuse with berries
paints the river's edge.
I listen to what the greater language hides.
My heart takes note.

I wanted them all and then
I wanted none. Wanted
to make it right, then knew
I could only settle
by choosing dignity.

Now I refuse the bloodied hands,
eat what my culture offers up,
and part one curtain of contradiction
as another returns
my beggar's stare.

Stuffing the Bird

Your turkey or roaster must be young, plump,
you must not think about its early death
but only savor the delight
it will coax shyly from your tongue.
Rub its body cavity and neck
with cumin, paprika, and cilantro,
a whiff of salt, pepper,
and hot cayenne, all soaked
in olive oil—a basting both pungent and thick.

Stuff your bird with toasted squares of
homemade bread tossed with chopped onion,
garlic, pine nuts, rosemary, and thyme, its
heart and liver minced and fried in melted butter.
Scoop the seeds of 2 ripe pomegranates and add
with their passion juice.
The liquid expands this mixture before
you loosely fill the coated cavities,
sew or skewer, then bake in covered clay,
20 minutes per pound.

Brown by uncovering the last half hour.
Thanksgiving or Christmas
or perhaps no holiday but intimate song,
the desire of your species craves selection,
a power that breeds its own excuse:
"If I don't eat this animal,
someone surely will."
One day the tiny tracks upon the sand
may speak your language.

Now share your special dinner
with the street-corner family
whose sign begs work for food, another day.

Ingredients
12- to 15-pound turkey
1 teaspoon cumin
1 teaspoon paprika
1 teaspoon cilantro
1 teaspoon salt
1 teaspoon pepper
1 teaspoon hot cayenne
1/2 cup olive oil
1/2 to 1 cup water to moisten the filling

Mud of Heaven

for Stan Persky

My friend Stan has just published a book
about the fall of European Communism,
ordinary household objects failing
to keep the promises we demand of them.

He knows that eros is the beginning
of knowledge.
His young lovers are hustlers
not prostitutes, entrepreneurs not victims.
As he is not their victimizer.

Stan's male homo culture is neither backdrop
nor center stage for his explanation
of what gave way, finally, what fumbles now,
rebirthing itself at Tirana's Dajti
or along the dissolving streets of Budapest.

"I have sort of stopped eating meat and pastries
though I don't yet notice any dramatic
shape difference," he writes me,
then asks if I have a poem
or recipe for chocolate mousse,
the Mud of Heaven as he calls it.

To Berlin's Fuggerstrasse I send instructions:
Sliver 6 squares semisweet chocolate,
a toss of salt and 2 tablespoons water
in a double boiler.
Stir until the chocolate is
meltdown smooth, a liquid lust.

Then beat 4 egg yolks to a light lemon color,
slowly combining with the chocolate.
Stir in 2 teaspoons vanilla extract
and beat the egg whites
with full knowledge of the task,
so they stand in soft peaks, yearning for sky.

Fold into the chocolate. Whip
and add your heaviest cream.
Spoon this Mud of Heaven into glasses
chilled until ready to serve.
More cream may be laced with sugar
and piled on top.

Six to eight hungry lovers satiate themselves
in this stirring and melting,
beating and whipping and yearning
and folding and spooning and cooling.
The fall of communism layers upon the tongue
in all its parts.

The memory of a young boy's back,
a statement of purpose
folded against the storm.

Hunger's Table

pain is not a flower, pain is a root
—Paul Monette

Now they sleep with the plague
beneath their pillows:
dancers and teachers, doctors and florists,
truckers and lawyers and priests.
Now they duel with her night sweats,
remembering that they will soon forget,
and die with our love in tow.

> The woman I was
> keeps setting this table,
> announces she is putting
> forks to the left,
> knives and spoons to the right,
> petals of night bloom
> curling.

Your skin tells time, a map
inviting me to contemplate
the loss of gardens.
There is no choice when choice
commands you turn your back on passion.
Lover and teacher, writer and friend,
come sit at my table
while you are still able to dine
and a canyon wren floats transparent song.

Water glasses are Mexican green,
wine goblets rimmed in fire,
dishes perfectly empty.
The woman I am
kicks off her shoes,
sits down to eat.
She thinks about
what taunts her on the plate,
devours its body,
repeats its name.

These are the years of love letters
written in granite
protruding over gentle hills.
One beside another,
and another, stones
that remind us you were here.

This is our defiant rainbow,
its broken stump still hidden
within the darkness of the storm.
Brother let me keep you company,
rub your tired feet. Let me
see you home.

> The woman I will be
> invites good friends to table.
> Serves memory's food.
> Tells stories
> between the soup course
> and her dream time.
> Holds a granddaughter on her lap
> and flies.

Hunger's table is unreachable in waiting,
its settings embrace discordant music,
noises that fill the head,
dishes bone clean and scraped,
a sound that courts the pain
of these brave times.

Welcome to our dear ghosts,
men whose historic flesh
plumps once-emaciated features,
who discreetly lift a saucer,
remarking upon its place and date
of fabrication.

Our brothers have forged
a terrible river.
Return has made them
more than hungry now.

Hannah's Stuffed Cabbage

I have no recipe, no story
from Hannah's kitchen to my own.
The Trial of the Century recedes
for just this afternoon
and it's Super Bowl Sunday.
Domestic violence—is it up or down?
the commentator asks.

Two California teams play to the
fatty sizzle of chile dogs and fries.
Those voices, heated shouts from the stands,
rising for one side or the other,
rise too in your body
and in mine.

For we are drawn like magnets to Susan Smith,
her babies drowned
in a lake of mother's madness.
The corpses in Chechnya and Bosnia,
Ulster and Haiti and Central LA.

In thick dreams I wade knee-deep
to where my great-aunt lets
the loosened leaves of cabbage
slip into a pot of boiling water,
then hands them quickly to cold.
Three or four minutes is all she needs
and they are soft, impressionable.

She makes the filling from chopped walnuts,
cooked white rice, minced parsley,
2 eggs and a handful of bread crumbs.
Salt and pepper to taste.
The mass should be light but hold together.

If we still ate meat, this would be
a different poem.
I have switched stations now.
Brahms rises to silence the kickoff,
those guns, people running for shelter
and from cold.

Flattening each cabbage leaf, she still teaches me
to cut a V from its tough root end
then carefully fold and roll
the leaf outward around its phrase of filling.

I take it from there,
arrange them in a shallow baking dish
side by side—soldiers who have rebelled
against their orders to kill.

If there is filling left
I spoon it among the rolls.
Then I pour stock or water
around the cabbage, dot with butter,
and sprinkle with sweet paprika.

This dish bakes at 350 degrees
for 1/2 hour
or until the scent of cooking cabbage
returns the stories
that give us back our lives.

Consider Lesbos

In *Like Water for Chocolate*, Pedro brought pink roses for Tita. She clasped them so tightly they turned deep red with the blood from her hands and breast. This love between a man and a women gallops across the screen, consuming itself in fire and in the art of cooking dishes that whet the mouth's juices, burn indelible in an audience of hungry *soldaderas*. Or, we may imagine *we* are the *soldaderas,* all of us riding that Mexican landscape, cooling our heels only when the lights come on.

Tita's six small quail nestle on a bed of twelve red roses, an equal number of chestnuts, butter, cornstarch, anise, honey, garlic, pitaya seeds, and two perfect drops attar of roses. I will not tell you how to prepare this delicacy. Mine is a different story. It belongs to women who love women, like Tita and Pedro but differently. The same but different. We are the *soldaderas* too, and everywhere in your audience, waiting for the scent of quail at table. Here is our recipe:

Heat 4 tablespoons olive oil in a large casserole. Sauté 8 trussed quail until they are browned, then transfer the birds to a waiting platter. They will slumber peacefully. In the same casserole, place 20 very small pearl onions, 1 bulb garlic (separated and peeled), 3 carrots scraped and quartered lengthwise, and 1 well-washed leek. When the onions are wilted, add bay leaves, fresh parsley sprigs, thyme, salt, pepper, a celery stalk with all its leaves, and a pinch of saffron.

Stir in 1/2 cup red wine vinegar, 2 cups dry white wine, and 1/2 cup fatless chicken broth. Return the quail to the casserole. Cover and simmer gently for 45 minutes. When done, remove from heat and arrange in a shallow earthenware dish. Pour cooking liquid over the birds, and allow to cool. Cover and refrigerate 3 to 4 days, turning occasionally.

For some, our knowledge opens with our lives. For others, it comes with the living—slow but nonetheless a gift. To serve, bring the dish to room temperature and, with scissors, cut the quail in halves for easier eating. Discard the leek, parsley, and celery. Julienne the cooked carrots and reserve. Return the quail skin-side up to the marinade and arrange with the carrots, pearl onions, thin slices of lemon, fresh parsley sprigs, and strips of red pepper.

We ask only that you taste this dish, served at room temperature, free from the demands or regrets of men. If you clear your mind of fear, and pull from memory the woman-loving women of your history, no one will place you where you do not want to be. You may come and go at your pleasure, free to choose. Choice—a central platter, not a condiment.

Sandra's Poor People's Recipes

Without a wife to make his tortillas, Grandpa Cordero had to learn how to make them himself. Sandra Cisneros tells me this story which is hers: the maternal grandfather who survived three major wars, one in Spanish and two in English, not to mention the Great Depression and Grandmother Anguiano's death. He had to learn how to make his own and he did—big dusty towers of flour tortillas hot off the comal.

You tell me you remember sitting on newspapers in the kitchen, wondering why there were always newspapers on the chairs. Grandpa serving his tortillas, and the kitchen always dark. Because Grandpa Cordero didn't believe in wasting electricity.

Homemade tortillas usually eaten with butter and salt, but sometimes your grandpa would get fancy. And you give me two recipes from that time, poor people's recipes, you say. One is for Peanut Butter Tacos, their two ingredients flour tortillas—never corn!—and peanut butter, any brand. You heat up your tortilla on a griddle if you want it crispy, in the microwave or over the range if you like it soft. Spread peanut butter while the tortilla is hot, fold in half, eat, and then say, *"¡Ay, qué rico!"*

Fried Bologna Tacos is your other memory. For these you fry the bologna in a pan until it puffs up like little hats, then place it on heated flour tortillas, add mustard (which must be French's—never Grey Poupon), and eat. Now the proper response is: Too delicious for words!

Sandra, you have your flour tortillas and peanut butter or bologna. I have my canned tuna fish, white bread, and processed cheese. We have both traveled far from our childhoods, eaten in restaurants with slender-stemmed goblets and too many forks to the left of the plate, linen that smells of dress code and five stars.

Still, we hold to these old tastes, the foods that remind us who we are. We will not wipe their temperature from our lips.

Onion Soup

In a large earthenware soup pot—no home
should be without one—the wife puts
about 8 pounds of good butter.
She browns a dozen large onions

chopped fine, and as many cloves of garlic,
stirring continuously with a wooden spoon.
Clay and wood in the kitchen, this is
a call to return, a plea

for remembrance, a song to be sung, softly.
She adds as much good wheat flour
as the butter will absorb,
salts and peppers strongly.

Everything here is larger than life, the mark
of intentionality. You can do this too.
Work the mixture as long as possible
until it turns a thick paste,

then press into a pot or tinned box
and cover tightly.
Allow to cool. Toulouse-Lautrec tells us
with this preparation in the high mountains

one can make thirty soups, allowing
a large spoonful of the mixture
per hunter.
Yes, we are speaking of hunters,

of altitude and glacial streams.
The spoonfuls are to be ladled
into a kettle with water
from the glaciers or the snow.

Boil for several minutes, then soak bread
previously toasted in front of the fire.
"This soup is made to carry
when hunters keep to the mountains

for a fortnight,
and to fortify people in a state of exhaustion,
no longer hungry but only thirsty,
who sleep out of doors at nine thousand feet."

Today's hunters are always hungry, and thirsty too.
They rarely sleep out of doors.
Two drove their pickup into Harry's Liquors
on the road between Chama and Tierra Amarilla,

took turns posing and using a Polaroid
on two majestic stags,
their broken bodies gashed red,
tongues trailing the forest betrayal.

The older of the two arranged the head
of his five-point buck,
the younger held a rifle across his chest.
No onion soup for these men,

only proud antlers and dead eyes in the den,
more snapshots pinned to a wall,
cold french fries tossed by the wife
when she cleans the refuse of their hunt.

Men telling the stories
we must counter with our own.

The Staff of Life

Into the bottomless space his invasion left
back when your resistance took a turn
toward sublimation,
dissolve dry yeast in lukewarm water.
This sea throws up a tangle of passwords
on its beach.

Stir in honey, molasses, or brown sugar,
dry milk if milk is what you drink.
Add whole wheat flour and beat well
with a wooden spoon, 100 strokes.

No beating was necessary to seal your lips
back then, only the steel promise
of his gentleman's eyes.
Let rise until doubled in volume
and in meaning.
One day the rising of your rage
will dissolve the fear,
I promise you this.

But when you fold in salt and oil, your heart
may harden into rifts of terror.
By adding 2 cups white flour and
another of wheat, you
slowly build the mass you need
to "get on with life."

It is wrongly your responsibility—to clean
his image with strong forearms,
kneading fingertips.
Slapping and gathering in the dough
is an exercise in pain control.
You have it now, have earned it

with a life remembered and cherished
as bread from the fire
calms this cusp of years.
We are always as strong
as our waiting need demands.

First rising: 50 to 60 minutes,
second 40 to 50.
Between them make a fist and punch
the risen dough, but gently.
Remember, this is your food, not his face
flattened by dust and the sifting of time.

Shape loaves in greased pans
and let rise one last breath of air:
20 minutes to 1/2 hour will do.
Finally, brush with a wash
of cold water or milk and egg.
Then bake. 350 degrees
for 25 minutes or until golden brown.

Remove from pans and cool
or eat right away.
Eat right away.

Ingredients
2 packages dry yeast dissolved in 3 cups lukewarm water
1/4 cup honey, molasses, or brown sugar
1 cup dry milk, optional
4 cups whole wheat flour
4 teaspoons salt
1/3 cup oil
2 cups unbleached white flour
1 cup whole wheat flour

The Buttermilk Bread Answers Back

For the bread's texture to stretch and sound
it is not enough to work the dough
carefully,
or add the last of the flour slowly,
a steady rhythm
drumming from the flat of your palms
to its resistant mass.

You must think about this bread, think
of its response between your hands.
Feel it reflecting your horror
of those men and women
in their gatherings of blasphemy.

Hayden Lake, Idaho. July 1995.
Beneath whispering pines
the Church of Jesus Christ
of the Christian Aryan Nations,
their Sieg Heil salutes
and burning crosses.

Mr. von Wolff mutters
and reporters hear his words.
"I wish we were marching you into the showers,"
he says. Chambers
made to look like what they were not.
An illusion, but for whom?

Told now as then, with attention
to these freedoms we hold dear.
The freedom to assemble.
The freedom to speak.
The rhythm of your wrists
must measure horror as a question,
visceral pain
only the surface of what lies beneath.

Good people live ordinary lives
upon that Idaho countryside.
Good people,
neighbors of those others
who believe themselves chosen.
And who choose.

This bread dough is more than the sum
of its particulars:
yeast, sugar, and warm water,
butter and buttermilk,
honey, salt, and flour.
More than what is called up
or bled or coaxed or shunned
on this windy summer day.

You slap the living spores and
pull them back, slap them again
and gather them up,
holding the leavened mass
in hands that ache for answers,
cry for an end to those chambers
and their crooked lies.

Bread, to grow committed
and unafraid,
must understand these things:
what we live with, what is acceptable,
what not.

From Cell to Cell

*for Judith McDaniel, and in gratitude to Barbara Deming
and so many others*

"Friends—strawberry Bavarian cream.
1 package frozen strawberries, 2 envelopes gelatin,
1/4 cup cold water or milk, 1/4 cup sugar,
2 eggs, 1 heaping cup crushed ice, 1 cup cream.
Defrost berries and heat 1/2 cup juice to simmer…"

Coming up on twenty days of fast, bodies weaken
but resolve continues strong.
A prisoner shouts the recipe from a newspaper,
discovers *it helps to talk about food,*
denial not part of her body politic.

Ingredients sung light-headed through
confinement of steel, wailing a language
those whose hearts are elsewhere cannot understand.
As it comes back around it breaks
against the walls that cannot hold.

Macon, Georgia: women and men imprisoned
limp-bodied but sure of spirit.
Arrested for walking peacefully
in support of the dignity of nations and of races.
Nineteen sixty-four, so much work to be done.

Twenty years later one of the women will remember:
"Though I did, yes,
share much with those earlier comrades,
much, too, was left *un*shared among us.
I never told them I was a lesbian."

One struggle no easier to reconcile
than the other.
To destroy capitalism. To destroy patriarchy.
Still pummeling the legacies
from those earlier battles, I honor the words

of this recipe defying a taste bud yearning
racist jailers cannot silence
then or now.
The woman who refuses the sad dictum:
If you do not speak its name, it will go away.

"Defrost berries and heat a half-cup juice to simmer…"

Soft But Firm

In her hut on the bank of the Río Magdalena
María Constancia sets the largest bowl
before the father of her boys and girls.
Rice and beans with their dark green sprig

of sweet cilantro. Moist air, aroma
of sustenance. *Señor, perdónannos
nuestros pecados...* Then come the bowls
for Eduardo and Daniel, Filiberto and Jaime

and little Martín. All the men. All her men
served in order of their size—
diminished compliance
through the patience of this August day.

Soak the beans. Hours of cooking will make them
soft but firm, with plenty of liquid
to be blended with the rice
which takes their color, brown of earth.

Elena, Bertita, and Concha quiet their hunger
on the run
as they move from cooking fire
to table and back. They do not sit.

The men require their taste buds free
from this rhythm of service,
double fare.
Daughters prepare their future toil,

pat tortillas between the palms
of generous hands—fold them
into the daily cloth, torn but clean.
They follow the route to those who eat

as they learn to serve. And serve again.
In Cleveland and Pocatello...
the Bronx...Scarsdale...Detroit...
Gladys orders the menu's best, smiles

then heads for the isolation
of a toilet stall. Flushes quickly.
Rinses her mouth. Or gobbles two Milky Ways
before the midtown tunnel

spews her into light again,
tosses their wrappers through the window,
rapid down and up,
a clockwork evidence.

Now she measures her lunch in ounces—
a carrot, a thimbleful of soup.
Worried she'll never be thin enough.
For working women the pressure cooker

reduces the preparation of beans to an hour
instead of a day. Fast food in place of a meal.
Calories, not taste, invade our story here,
the mutant recipe.

We serve with the size of our bodies
or we fade from sight.
María Constancia and Gladys
inhabit a single cell of shape and sound.

How full they are. How absent.
How pale we grow.

Angélica's Black Mole* Oaxaqueño

for Angélica's Mexican Cafe in Ybor City, Florida

This is a story of icons, a story of Frida's
dark eyebrows joined in grace, her gaze
touching us still, and of the Virgin of Guadalupe
supported here by a Náhuatl angel of memory.

This is a poem of women's memory and work, Dorothy
bringing us together, Angélica's kitchen gleaning
its history from Iris and Diana, Ruth as messenger
and Margaret offering her poems beneath a canopy of trees.

Beneath these trees, charango and guitar lift Barbara's
voice back to the grandmother cooks, *sabias*
of our dancing histories. Sisters and strangers,
we rinse our hands beneath the ritual stream, these

hands that are brown and black and white, ready
to remove the stems, the seeds and veins
from 1/4 pound black ancho chiles, 2 ounces
each pasilla and guajillo chiles, toasted and soaked

*Mole, pronounced mo-lay.

30 minutes in cold water. Toast seeds until
they blacken, then cover with more cold water,
5 minutes is all we need before removing to the
blender jar. Add 1 large broiled tomato, 3 cloves,

3 whole allspice, 1/4 teaspoon thyme and another
of ground marjoram, 1 tablespoon Mexican oregano, and
1 cup water. Heat 1/2 cup safflower oil, using it
to fry and drain l/4 cup sesame seeds,

1/4 cup peanuts, 10 almonds, 1/4 cup raisins, 1 small
thickly sliced onion, 12 peeled garlic cloves,
1 slivered cinnamon stick, and 3 slices dried bread.
All come to our blender jar with water as needed

and now we need the passion of 2 ounces Mexican chocolate
combined with the magic of chiles roasted in prehistory.
One fourth cup safflower oil in a heavy saucepan
pulls ingredients up to a medium flame,

a flame that lifts them all to aromatic brown. Stir
and scrape. Blend chiles with water, add the chocolate
and cook for 6 minutes, exactly 6. Our bodies
move together in this kitchen. We count a chorus of

heartbeat, a chorus of memory when the mind falls
free. Now add 4 cups water (or chicken broth
if no one has moved from the animal path).
Cook another 35 minutes until thick and

when thickened salt to taste. The salt of our tears,
the rock of our hands as they work in unison,
battles cut corners, solutions too real
to be eaten in mixed company.

In the company of pink corn tortillas gently warmed
before folding around a strip of yellow cheese,
soft tacos on a low-fired plate, just dipped
in the mole, a centerpiece for rice and beans.

Rice and beans: our ancient call to arms, the mole
that passes from one to another woman's life,
grandmother to mother, mother to daughter
to the sister you loved in a time before burnt pots

and pots of unknown metals chilled your groping.
We are only as new as the taste of a
lover's tongue, as patiently old
as the place we're coming from.

Rice Pudding

If the mind stops
there is always rice pudding.
My father's Alzheimer's
was a word we never spoke.
It cradled our terror
like flame
ready to close the throat,
pull memory down to ash.

A handful of rice
and lots of water.
Nothing measured
demands your spent attention.
When he opened his mouth
the sentences would not line up,
refused
to hold their own.

I wondered
if there was a moment
beyond which nothing wept or strained
against the tide.
A stick of cinnamon,
curled about his hope.
After boiling to consistency—
a little sugar, perhaps some milk.

Rice pudding is
the ease with which you concede
the journey, nothing more
is up to you.
Nothing predictable.
To live without sure knowledge,
yes or no,
is my inheritance.

This and his years of love,
first home,
once living eyes
disappearing into the final cage of bone.

Exorcism

Two dark wings, heartbeat of feathers.
Or will it be a breast this time,
surgically cornered
to block the known caress?

A puzzle of words crosses your silence.
Breathing becomes a code.
Of ease, only random numbers
remain.

You must fix anchor to this beating
of anticipated days.
Follow the blood
fresh beets deposit on the knife.

Stained fingers
lift them from the cooking pot,
steal them from heat, bathe them
so that touch is possible.

Finger the skins
that shear beneath a steady stream.
Clean and slice.
Discard remaining grit

until the memory of their plumpness calls.
Neither armored nor worn
but futured in their perfect egos,
roots to be pared

as thin as the pages in this book of chance.
Add the translucence of onion,
white against wine.
Balsamic vinegar, a bit of oil and salt.

Each minute brings its story.
Each new fear this adventure of wings.

Notes

Grape Pie

César Chávez led the United Farm Workers, which organized migrant laborers working in the vineyards and picking other seasonal crops in California and throughout the western United States.

Shirley's Kugel

This is a recipe from Shirley Melvin, extraordinary businesswoman, mother, grandmother, and social activist in the Philadelphia area.

Canyon Food

We traveled 286 miles of the Colorado River by dory through the Grand Canyon in June and July of 1995. Ceramicist Dennise Gackstetter was our expedition cook.

Squash Blossom Budín

This recipe and the history that moves with it are from *Frida's Fiestas: Recipes and Reminiscences of Life with Frida Kahlo* by Guadalupe Rivera and Marie-Pierre Colle (New York: Clarkson-Potter, 1994).

Coatlicue was the Aztec goddess of earth, or earth mother. Much like Christianity's Virgin Mary, she conceived miraculously. But the similarity ends there. The left-handed warrior Huizilopochtli impregnated her with a feather, raising the wrath of her four hundred sons and oldest daughter, all of whom he had to slay. Her ferocious stone facsimile can be seen in Mexico City's National Anthropology and History Museum.

Cleora's Dream

This poem is written with gratitude to *Cleora's Kitchens: The Memoir of a Cook & Eight Decades of Great American Food* by Cleora Butler (Tulsa, Oklahoma: Council Oak Books, Ltd., 1985).

Migration of Seasons

A point of departure for this poem was "The Nazi Treatment of Animals and People" (*Reinventing Biology* by Lynda Birke and Ruth Hubbard, Bloomington and Indianapolis: Indiana University Press, 1995) by Arnold Arluke and Boria Sax. Their essay documents the ways in which the elite of Germany's National Socialist Party revered and protected animals while systematically brutalizing and murdering millions of human beings. From that essay, and among much else, I learned that Hitler's dog was named Blondi. Also interesting was Jane Kramer's "The Politics of Memory" in *The New Yorker Magazine* (August 14, 1995, pp. 48–65).

Hannah's Stuffed Cabbage

The Trial of the Century refers to the O.J. Simpson murder trial that captured the U.S. public's attention for more than a year of almost constant TV and radio broadcasts. The other news items referred to in this poem are from the same time period.

Consider Lesbos

Like Water for Chocolate is a best-selling novel by Laura Esquivel (English translation by Carol and Thomas Christensen, New York: Doubleday, 1992). It is also a motion picture, released by Miramax. Esquivel is one of the first writers to successfully combine recipes with fiction in a large-audience book. My poems pay her tribute.

The women who fought in the 1910 Mexican revolution were called *soldaderas*.

Hunger's Table
This poem emerges from the terrifying and inspiring AIDS era.
Paul Monette's quote is from "Gardenias" in *Love Alone, Eighteen Elegies for Rog* (New York: St. Martin's Press, 1988).

Onion Soup
The recipe in this poem is from *The Art of Cuisine* by Henri de Toulouse-Lautrec and Maurice Joyant. (Translated by Margery Weiner; first published in Great Britain by Michael Joseph Ltd.)

From Cell to Cell
The history for this poem can be found in *Prisons That Could Not Hold* by Barbara Deming (Athens, Georgia, and London: University of Georgia Press, 1995).

Angélica's Black Mole Oaxaqueño
Early in the process of writing the poems for this book, I read some of the first ones outside Angélica's Mexican Café in Ybor City, Florida. It was September 16, 1995, and we were celebrating Mexico's independence from Spain. The audience gathered at tables under the trees in the walkway in front of the café, talking eagerly about their own relationships to food. Some later wrote to me, and one even sent a copy of a southern-style kosher cookbook. Angélica Díaz consented to share her recipe for black mole, which she said Iris Noble adapted from Diana Kennedy's *The Art of Mexican Cooking* (New York: Bantam Books, 1989).

About the Author

MARGARET RANDALL, well-known in feminist and literary circles, has authored over seventy books, predominantly about women and women's experiences, both in the U.S. and in Latin America, where she spent much of her adult life. She received the first Lillian Hellman and Dashiell Hammett grant to writers victimized by political persecution in 1990, and in 1989 one of her essays was cowinner of the Mencken Freedom at Risk Award. A photographer and social activist as well as a poet, oral historian, and author, she lectures extensively all over the country. She lives with her partner in Albuquerque, New Mexico.

More Papier-Mache Press Titles of Related Interest

I Am Becoming the Woman I've Wanted
Edited by Sandra Haldeman Martz

Winner of a 1995 American Book Award, *Becoming* focuses on how women feel about their bodies and the broader question of how the physical aspects of being female affect women's experiences. In the emotionally evocative style that has characterized Martz's collections, women delve into a broad range of personal experiences, from coming of age and budding sexuality to the physical changes and challenges that accompany growing older.

"Tending toward the emotive and always from the subjective, these pieces articulate what it is like to be Everywoman from every age." —Library Journal

ISBN 0-918949-49-1, trade paper
ISBN 0-918949-50-5, hardcover

Washing the Stones: Selected Poems 1975–1995
Maude Meehan

A well-respected activist and California poet, seventy-five-year-old Maude Meehan speaks eloquently for her generation. Chronicling one woman's journey, Meehan's poetic memoir of passion, love, and politics commemorates the experiences of a life lived fully, with her partner of fifty-seven years, and after his death.

*"These poems celebrate family, children, and long years of sensual love. The exemplary title poem, 'Washing the Stones,' particularly speaks of loss and continuity." —*Grace Paley, author of *The Collected Stories*

ISBN 0-918949-85-8, trade paper

Like a Summer Peach:
Sunbright Poems and Old Southern Recipes
Edited by Blanche Flanders Farley and Janice Townley Moore

This charming collection unites luscious poems revolving around food with corresponding enticing recipes, complemented by Deidre Scherer's rich textile images. Like the fortune in a cookie, this captivating book inspires personal insights, as the poems impart both humorous and serious emotional ties with food, enriching the pleasure of favorite foods. Many of the recipes are traditionally Southern.

"From the region of soul food comes this wonderful book of food for the soul."
—Pat Conroy, author of *Beach Music* and *The Prince of Tides*

ISBN 0-918949-89-0, hardcover

Kitchen Tables (and Other Midlife Musings)
Niela Eliason

Niela Eliason captures the lively essence of daily life and its accompanying memories for anyone in their midlife years. These essays are a treasure chest of the insightful thoughts, feelings, and opinions of our middle-aged generation—trusting chicken soup, staying married, and sharing stories around the kitchen table.

"Have a seat at Niela Eliason's kitchen table. You'll enjoy the stories she's going to tell you" —Tony Hillerman

ISBN 0-918949-62-9, trade paper

Papier-Mache Press

At Papier-Mache Press, it is our goal to identify and successfully present important social issues through enduring works of beauty, grace, and strength. Through our work we hope to encourage empathy and respect among diverse communities, creating a bridge of understanding between the mainstream audience and those who might not otherwise be heard.

We appreciate you, our customer, and strive to earn your continued support. We also value the role of the bookseller in achieving our goals. We are especially grateful to the many independent booksellers whose presence ensures a continuing diversity of opinion, information, and literature in our communities. We encourage you to support these bookstores with your patronage.

We publish many fine books about women's experiences. We also produce lovely posters and T-shirts that complement our anthologies. Please ask your local bookstore which Papier-Mache items they carry. To receive our complete catalog, send your request to Papier-Mache Press, 135 Aviation Way, #14, Watsonville, CA 95076, or call our toll-free number, 800-927-5913.

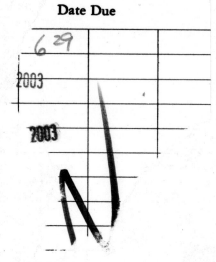